The Rest Is Silence

POEMS

by

Tafadzwa Chiwanza

First published in Great Britain in 2024 by:

Carnelian Heart Publishing Ltd

Suite A

82 James Carter Road

Mildenhall

Suffolk

IP28 7DE

UK

www.carnelianheartpublishing.co.uk

Paperback ISBN   978-1-914287-79-4

eBook ISBN   978-1-914287-80-0

Edited by Memory Chirere

Cover design:

Artwork – 'Palindrome' (2024), by Samantha Rumbidzai Vazhure

Layout - Rebeca Covers

Interior:

Typeset by Carnelian Heart Publishing Ltd

Layout and formatting by DanTs Media

Here is what you do with grief: foreword to The Rest is Silence

I met Tafadzwa Chiwanza for the first time in my office in 2019 when I was still a lecturer in the then Department of English at the University of Zimbabwe. He just walked in with a fellow Accounting student and spent close to an hour talking to me about the craft of poetry, all the while evincing the demeanour of someone who was eager to observe and archive. He was meeting me for the first time after months of conversing with the skeletons of my mind in the Edward Dzonze-manned Poetry Intercourse WhatsApp group. The group allowed us to spend some time conversing about poetry and indulging in poetry duets. The intercourse group was more of a dumping ground for poets who could not wait for their poems to constitute a collection before getting them out there. Poems were composed on the spur of the moment and indiscriminately thrown into the group for our restless minds to munch on. It was riotous, but in that riot, we found a home. A year after our meeting, Chiwanza would go on to read excerpts from *No Bird is Singing Now?* (2020) at Mama JC's birthday.

Those who have read *No Bird Is Singing Now?* will tell you that the real meaning of *No Bird is Singing Now?*, it seems, is found in the poet attempting to come to terms with the fact that we are but transient creatures, born merely to die. The world began, as Chiwanza remembers, with a word, with a newborn's cries attracting ululations from perspiring midwives, but ends with "broken silence". This knowledge that one day the persona will transition from being to non-being makes him struggle to come to terms with the fact that we are but "infected wounds/Inside the giant clay nostrils of time." However, in *The Rest Is Silence*, the poet is grappling with the loss of another. It is for this reason that *The Rest Is Silence* can be read as one huge poem. In saying this, I do not want to mislead the reader into thinking that the relentlessness with which the poet focuses on loss is like flogging a dead horse. Far from it! There is a narrative to this collection which oscillates between love and loss, and the complex emotions that are aroused by these. To love is to lose and to grieve. Thus, where in *No Bird Is Singing Now?* the poet thinks of his death with trepidation – what if his lover runs into the arms of another soon after his interment? – in *The Rest Is Silence* the flipside is of the poet remaining in the world devoid of a loved one.

In focusing on this, Chiwanza avoids the mournful tone that one finds in many Shona poems that focus on death. Instead, there is a Yeatsian tinge to Chiwanza's approach, but where Yeats sounds like an acquaintance in 'Upon a Dying Lady', choosing instead to wittily observe and not to feel, Chiwanza is involved. He is metaphorically dying with her. When that happens, grief will make one "poke the moon" or "put the reeds of the sky together/ and make a tiny mat" on which one will spend the rest of one's days in silence.

Chiwanza's sensitivity to death is not accidental. He was born in Hurungwe, Mashonaland West province. His mother told him that it was in the morning. He was born in a hut and his grandmother was the midwife. His mother didn't know she was carrying twins, so after his brother was born, the midwife was alarmed because she felt something in his mother's womb. Chiwanza's grandfather quickly ran to a Sangoma who lived nearby and he was told that there was another child in the womb. That's how he was born. According to his mother, Chiwanza came out small as a mouse and was not expected to live. After losing his father in his early teens, Chiwanza escaped to poetry in an attempt to cope with his sense of loss. There was something in creating poetry that answered to his urgent need. Poetry allowed him to create a world in which his father remained a constant presence. At the University of Zimbabwe in 2018, Chiwanza found himself in a place whose sheer size and impenetrability isolated him. He felt lost and inconsequential and found solace in reading dense theoretical iterations that one finds in Rousseau or Derrida. At the University of Zimbabwe, these are famously located in Stackroom 4 of the University Library. The jungle of books in there is so thick that one can hide for years without being discovered. One day, Chiwanza escaped into the popular Stackroom 2 of the library where he was soon swallowed by its forest of books, including shelf upon shelf of poetry books. That's how we eventually met. We met at a time when, for Chiwanza, creating poetry had ceased to be a mode of survival and had morphed into the way he could see the world around him better – lenses on the peak of a mountain, as he would say. It was also during this time that I was attempting to trace sadness back to its source so that in Chiwanza I found a precocious young friend with whom I could have conversations about my vision of poetry. However, it is Chiwanza's vision in *The Rest Is Silence* that has me in awe.

In this collection, Chiwanza's sharp intellect, eye for detail and surprising choice of metaphors stand out. But it is also his intentional unveiling of what it means to watch the imminent arrival of death and loss that enables this collection to have a unity of effect. All the poems are working towards that singular effect, so that long after you have gone through the collection, the echoes of it will continue to haunt you. Grief, in the hands of a poet of Chiwanza's capability, is as bewitching as the legendary brew of my grandmother, VaHarutyi, or, as Chiwanza the accountant would say, as bewitching as money itself!

Tanaka Chidora, author of Because Sadness is Beautiful? (2019)

"O, I die, Horatio.

…On Fortinbras. He has my dying voice.

So tell him, with th' occurrents, more and less,

Which have solicited. **The rest is silence***.*

O, O, O, O. (dies)"

Shakespeare, *Hamlet*

this collection crept out of me

like a sudden urge to sneeze.

Contents

No Bird is singing now?

Valerie's song

dust whirling with the wind

hurls memories in twirling chaos,

stench preceding rotting flesh

before the clock halts at Unknown o'clock:

time locked, mind flogged,

then the screaming!

eerie sounds from a wounded bull.

once the fool, at time's fullness still a fool,

a fool's gamble, caught in an enigma

a perpetual loop:

leaping from one ephemeral moment to another,

with a single song on replay,

relaying layers laid with heart's bricks,

pricking the soul when the ticking stops.

lost is the song in time, and time in the song.

between the crime and the victim

a silent matrimony to never kiss and tell,

but the stench of crime is dragged

as sunset drags darkness at his dusty heels…

the wounds are stories of cowardice

with multiple endings

ending whenever the stories start:

of Cupid's shiny dagger

bought for thirty pieces of silver,

and love, a blind wingless dove,

a taste of the moon's ashes

lashing with claws wherever blood glows in the dark.

off to the time then

when time was jealous

and the song was sung

from the forest beyond ordinary endings,

now Valerie's lost song

shrieks and wanders in limbo –

a wrecked flotilla captained by ghosts

rummaging the seas seeking rest.

the ringing in the ear is the song skin wrung

and hung out to dry,

I laid lies around her heart

in metal circles coated with chocolate.

the song I sang was hope,

now turned to ash as she sings it

forever together never again.

it's not nothingness that now remains

when everything has eloped with the wind,

the moon's effulgent embrace, the sun's heliacal kiss...

but I remain!

like the bones scattered at Golgotha,

as evidence of the crime committed against the criminal...

I remain to gather all the shiny pieces of regret

hastily ripped into multiple identities

all traceable to the works of my hands:

the potter despised by his own pottery!

when the song was written,

death was the mortal foe

each breath now heavy sighs,

and my armies march now against me

singing Valerie's song –

my song!

my words, and my foes,

now nigh and inseparable:

thick as thieves bound by blood,

my blood, they found common ground –

In search of ways to put my body in the ground...

I am not the victim!

the spinning journey spun this thick jacket of a song

whose threads thread deep into my veins.

It's in vain to rip it off –

the song has already been sung!

so here we are, at last

the last of multiple copies of whoever we were

daring not to wonder how we got here,

yet we know

the printer on auto-print

regurgitated copy after copy

of the self, shelving solipsism,

a bond binding two souls whittled away into smoke,

tatters of it scattered in the sky.

now our courses have reconverged,

not to glean the residual green the reapers left,

nor to heed the didactic teachings on the scars:

a rigmarole initiation into pain

all because of paean sung for a Writer's Muse.

the anfractuous course, an odyssey of choices,

choosing the noise over the voices

that whispered Valerie's song into existence,

the dung over the roses

whence the song sprung and was sung

deep into summer's warmth,

and fast past a thousand winter's wraths

wreaking through breezes and frozen rectus.

the alchemy that spoke the word of transformation

transported weary feet into wings,

flapping past nettles and thistles into the sunset,

and I a shrivelled sinner shriven of sin.

But the guilt

becomes the colour of my blood!

springing the sin in an ebullient flood:

thoughts of redemption with no penance

laugh at each other in my head –

gullible! The song sung must be heard;

fatuous! The sinner's fanciful hope

of escaping the wages of his trade.

However brusque the romance was, a sin is a sin –

only a head on the platter will suffice,

my head!

The past is a stubborn stain

22

on the lap of a dark street

on the lap of a dark street

her body lies.

Curious eyes ogling

between flapping sheets of night's clothing.

a single volunteer

near her half naked body willing to hunch…

she is still breathing.

her heart faint, almost numb as her mind.

Memories from a distant echo

ebb away, with the dim urban street lights

the sound of his voice. The noise,

the stench and the warmth of her blood

familiar.

But she has never been here before,

dying,

waiting for a salvation

only he can bring…

Patching the havoc

silence flowing like a river

all day long plunges headlong into a cup,

up goes the rain in quick march

into the arms of the austere sun,

spun around and shoved –

down the alimentary canal as ash.

the mural on the wall embellished with grotesques:

of temples queuing to quarrel,

and dreams with broken limbs lying askew,

and she, coughing in the next room.

a dagger deep in her stomach,

left to die in the street by an angry client,

giant hands from the other side

on standby by her side,

numb to the pained stench she is now –

the subliminal cold takes centre stage,

this stage the actress must exit…

absent applause.

Eyes' lingering gaze –

for long on the ground scattered –

finally gathered,

attending to the distant chatter of nurses

attending to her mortal wounds,

the words beyond the groping fingers of the ear,

eyes reading the lines written on their distant lips

the mind grasping a hastily made conclusion:

she's gone!

this woman – two breaths ago

to my heart a stranger –

summons snow and frost to my spine

(the thought of her death to me a death in itself)

to gather what's left when all strength is gone.

long and narrow is the receding path

between I and the truth of the woman's fate.

through the window terrified eyes peep,

then a beep…

She lives…

Patching particles of light

dismal

the medicinal stench of the hospital –

a marauder, waylaying my nose.

a subtle heave of her chest

smuggled through the backdoor of a dream –

dark as the emptiness behind sun's smiling face,

sudden substance

from chaos and commotion, commissioned.

strange is happiness

to the perennially wet cheek,

as is the stranger lying before eyes blurry,

who opens hers as if to wash the tears from mine:

"Kathy," her voice tickles the senses,

before sliding into the arms of the murky darkness

beneath the shut eyelids. But

I can save her…

An arrow through the head

days trickle through a cone shaped funnel

into the flask of Kathy's presence.

each night for a fortnight before her bed,

Cupid's arrow dashing through my head.

Crawling out of the hospital

in vain the contents of Kathy's mind

the mind tries to unpack

as her eyes are fixed on the water-stained walls,

and her feet crawl out of the hospital.

the past is a stubborn stain

the poem,

a cataract of words,

gothic worlds of

characters conceived from caricatures,

a universe apart from the path

of Plath's genius.

Kathy writes of grotesque eyebrows

eloping from withering faces,

"emblems of an ephemeral existence," says she

and the poem is dedicated to me.

its words are inscribed backwards –

a gigantic pedal into dusty arms of the nebula,

of meaning, sere meadows,

serial chaos, in comeliness abject poverty,

but of depth, constellations!

her deep dark past in the dismal streets of Harare

with scattered photons of light

attempts to dispel the gloom from her history:

but the path is a stubborn stain

the stain of a stubborn past

from which I must save her...

Kathy's hour of blankness

Last night Kathy failed to write,

the poem wrestled in her, daring to come out,

its words threatening to burst her asunder.

dark as the crown on the crow's head,

the poem formed a cow,

leaning on her spongy mind like two magnets:

Kathy's writer's block!

a dark blankness

carelessly scribed on the chalkboard

sizzled with learned rage from her specs –

specks of deafness, death

loss and grief,

common denominators

with nothing in common but the thought –

last of many –

chiselling what was left of her corroded mind.

But I must save her…

Kathy's Poem

the guitar strings drag
streams of nightmarish realities,
multiple packages of Kathy's faces.
masks tall as the wall of Berlin,
pile beneath her pillow
where all her effulgent dreams dimmed
and seemed to scream daggers made of ice,
her skin, a thin layer of melting candles
upon which time walked with feet made of needles –
a blast of wintry winds
through the no-man's land between *Then and Now!*

Kathy's cats catch not mice:
cannibals!
emblems of her eternal problems with the self…
the catechism into this religion!
the thud at the end of the drawn catapult
throttles her temple into my arms:
ruined. smashed. unholy incense
desecrated
by men needing satisfaction…

but I must save her…

writing on a night walk

down a path besieged by nettles,

where the sun is an occasional visitor,

the ineffable feet trudge

night into the thirsting ground

until steams of dust sizzle to form a thick porridge

from the dense air of this Nowhere.

cruel mind summons the sum of my grief:

a father gone and a sister perished!

Kathy and I

have tasted sun's ashes.

metric tonnes of celestial residue

dished like a debt from God long overdue,

to form from us a statue made of ash,

divorced of virtue:

a gothic farce of the devil's horns!

the tears of a crippled boy and a blind woman

crawl to trickle back to their home beneath the eyes,

before sight is engulfed in charcoal-black ice

cementing the demented question with a pregnant sigh.

grief, bliss' natural thief,

brief –

the nakedness

that clothes us when shadows grow cold:

a father gone and a sister perished!

Dark As Kathy's Dreams

the sun –

the burning end of a dying cigarette –

engulfed in a thick jacket of dark clouds

that swim over the vast expanse

above our grotesque shape of home.

Kathy's temple twirled in my arms:

in her sleep she shivers: there's snow in her dreams.

her skies are milk dipped in ash.

her memories are deep as mortal wounds.

her eyes weep gangrene and dust.

on the cheeks of the Avenues

her mind is stuck,

the foliage of the jacaranda trees

sentinel,

silent witnesses

to the horrors Kathy survived…

At the heels of Kathy's shadow

winter came and Earth took off its hat

to expose a head that resembled the aftermath of veld fires.

I had washed my skin in the sun that stained it

and hung it to dry.

Kathy, curled between my fingers like a wedding ring,

gazes at the bloodstains on her blouse:

a whisper through the damp fabric of time, collapsed on her lap.

the wintry darkness hides scars and shadows –

Kathy likes to slip under its armpits,

to wallow behind its spectre,

to escape the past that hunts her at the heels of her shadow.

Shadows that dissolve the sun

the filthiness crawls on her skin

with its greasy legs dipped in drums of memories,

the taste of dead smiles

scattered in the valley of her mind's mouth

in which morsels of disgust

lay hidden in the crevices between her teeth,

a falling leaf, her tongue tied,

witnesses molasses molested into ash.

this man, one of many, lust-driven, plunged

like a rock into the murky waters of her life,

choking and smacking her senseless,

now slouches from the bed, disgusted,

calls her a whore, throws two dollars at her

before vanishing into the depths of the night

like hundreds of men before him:

some would return, some would not,

but Kathy would always remember their faces.

Numb

the contents of her head turn to ash.

her brain decays in the chasm in her skull –

substanceless, *placeless* and plain as pain.

Kathy screams, scratches and digs her nails

deep into her skin to scrub the repulsion,

to murder the thought of this man

and those men that have desecrated her thighs.

the stench of regret lingers,

the walls of her tiny room leaning towards her

to cast shadows dark enough to dissolve the sun.

Kathy tells me about Keisha

memories, old as rain, drag seas through the door.

Kathy, distant, gazes through the wall

of misty time, separating

Then and Now.

her tongue a blunt spear, dulls

the ear with its tales

of Keisha from the Avenues

who could not be saved.

Keisha to Kathy, a dear sister. Grief

unfathomable. Shipwrecked and lost to the sea

of their former occupation.

The footsteps of the nightmares fade

Sun surrenders to night.

A wet darkness crawls to cover space and time

with a misty fur gently swaying on the skin,

an eerie touch from a ten-fingered hand…

spooky thoughts, and skittishness:

the two sons born of a dread of superstition

leap from night's deep pockets

as silent as darkness itself.

Goodnight

when at night no goodness remains:

the taste of a rock charred in fire for a thousand years

inveigles the taste buds

to make the rock taste like water

harrying the pink softness with rough edges

until the tongue hangs like a paper dipped in blood.

Night brings clarity with its darkness,

an endless oxymoron

perfectly balanced on imbalanced scales

like Kathy's laughter in her sleep as tears wet her pillow:

bliss and sadness: lovers locked in infernal shackles,

time, a beautiful misery!

tides of contrasting windy emotions tied to the hourglass

blow a trumpet of darkness through the jammed window:

before the candle melts into white ashes,

leaving glimmers on Kathy's cheeks...

weeping in her dreams for reasons to all unknown,

but with the time the concealed to be revealed,

yet clarity has never been revered –

often feared on its solitary reveries beyond human fallacies.

A miasma of confusion

poured through sun's deceptive rays

scatters into dust beneath night's consecration –

so do the masks all wear

at last in the dark the true self is exposed:

Eyes sullen, shoulders sagged and skin pale,

a vile caricature of a creature from a dark pit,

a spitting image of one's worst nightmare.

In the dark all must face their worst fears,

all but Kathy with eyes shut like Noah's ark

and a smile carved on a sleeping face.

Perhaps, she has been saved...

The emptiness when she is not

the silent walls
rose to their feet and left the house
utterly empty.

Kathy's memories
scurry to the gates of my mind
as the rain burns on my roof,
pitter-pattering on the windows of our future,
terrifyingly tearing eye's gaze from the ceiling
which at any time could grow wings.
the shiny floor
scatters into wrinkles beneath my feet –
brooks branching into veins
innumerable threads, only one leading her home:
a nameless, placeless place
in which my arms are the roof
softly absorbing the wrath of the battering rain,
and the warmth of my whispers
nestling in her soaked hair
spread like a towel on my lap,
nurses her, as the utter emptiness slowly fades

Perhaps she can save me too…

Lovely, in Kathy's arms

the window is slightly open

and a cool summer night wind whirls softly

like it's flirting with the idea of getting in.

In the room the air is a warm emptiness

like the hazy memory of a childhood scent

buried in the undying odours of a short life.

Her mountain-shaped chest heaves slowly

before she sighs happily,

her gaze dripping scented petals

with my name carved at their lip-shaped backs.

My gaze descends like a floating cloak

and rests in the comfort of her eyes.

Kathy tries to catch the dark

the days grow long and dreary

and their shadows march at time's ankles.

Kathy reaches into the dark

groping for something, some substance,

a fabric to clothe the empty moment

whose life seems to echo for centuries,

and I sit at this halcyon table,

watching her trying to catch the dark.

Kathy swims in the shadows

the past, ever so deep, spans its elastic jaws

to gobble the residues of Kathy's hopes.

the future, shallow, weakly flickers in her eyes.

with lungs drowning in a warm flood of her blood.

coughs, and the blood spatters on her mouth.

the monitor goes berserk, nurses bustle,

time, tussling in the clock's hands, coughs to a halt.

the stab wound between her ribs drips pus,

forming a yellow dam of thick opaque exudates.

life, a stranger to her face, dances in the distance

as Kathy swims in the shadows beneath the eyelids.

death and life brawl

in a silent bombardment of atomic explosions.

serenity, as nurses stare in pregnant expectation

before the monitor beeps back to life

and the sighs of the nurses shred the silence.

Kathy needed saving

deep in the dark depths of depression

Kathy, fragments of a frayed fabric

restless, wrestles to get out of her own head

where thoughts smoother tiny foetuses of her light.

all exit signs are traps –

doors scuttle from her stretched hands,

and the walls conspire to crumble upon her...

Oh! Kathy, how in your nightmare you call my name.

I, with a gun loaded, but unsure where to shoot.

Stygian lakes separating us grow more forbidding

as if to adumbrate inevitable doom.

the cold shadows cast from your side of the bed

chew at my hip –

the last gasps of a galloping horse.

Kathy – depressed, dying before my eyes –

opens hers to smile at me, as if to say:

you cannot save me...

Kathy's temple

The wind whistles through the window,

shattered. Ruined vestiges of life,

feet that walked on water trapped in glassy

ice. Dust. Flesh. Vignettes in a tragedy

scuffed and old flesh, decaying. Depreciating.

Kathy's temple dangles from the roof,

hair tousled, a dishevelled gothic beauty,

broken neck, eyes bulged,

the reek of her corpse rains to flood the room.

the stench of death crawls on the skin,

the sight pokes eyes from their sockets,

the thought! Oh Kathy, the thought,

a concrete beam leaning against the walls,

an upgrade of the Torturer's technique:

soft as pain, with a feather,

the Torturer tickles me to near death,

beneath Kathy's flapping dress.

locked around her body like chains,

the shackles this world was to her, her whole life:

Oh! Kathy, free at last thou art!

When she left him

his finger poked the moon,

its ashes stained his nails with its regrets,

the sun, miles of emptiness away,

stared indifferent with a face made of stone,

stars screamed at the scars on the tongue of time.

the rivers that flow between clouds

folded their arms

and the churning waters circled in the dams of their armpits,

before despair poured into earth's dry mouth.

the staring sun at last blinked darkness into life

and the ash turned to snow.

he, naked and destitute, put the reeds of the sky together

and made a tiny mat.

the stars popped out like buttons

into the arms of the emptiness after emptiness

which sat across the table

waving a burning cigarette at his ghost-white eyes

Memories of a smile

Outward man, perish!

(Another strange birthday)

a phalanx of wrinkles

in brisk march under my eyes,

hairline under siege

retreats to camp behind fontanels,

leaving no-man's-land **a** bare whaleback.

eyes, shot and wounded,

bleed out on a bloody stretcher

where many traded eyes for specs

to dare see the incandescent glare of old age.

my back crackles and aches

as ancient clocks herald dusty Time:

the companion of my youth

turned to mortal foe in my old age.

ears hear nothing short of gunshot decibels

as barefooted voices limp in my eardrums

to crimson dye my ears' fulvous fur.

my hands dance to polar temperatures

as my hepatic sense turns chaotic.

army tankers' barrels swivel,

ready to make my mucky nose snivel.

ever-dying fervent prayers and hopes

gallop to an early rest in Time's nest,

from Hamlet's ad hominem arguments

on whether to be or not be,

yet, that has never been the question for me.

The Milky Way in my cup

the night begins to smoke daylight,

and with each puff, the sun disappears into night's lungs

in which nicotine sits astride chewing darkness

while raunchy, voyeuristic stars applaud

before celestial passion explodes into fragile violence

to make the infinite skies a harbour of cloudy scars

wrapped in the dusty smoke of the milky way.

the galaxy from where I stand squirms in my cup.

I see it – a hazy band of light, recumbent against dark matter

floating in the scattered arms of tiny teabags –

before I guzzle the milk way down my alimentary canal:

a taste of the universe that tasted my flesh!

Memories of a smile

stout drops of yesterday's rain

slide like sweat from the tree's cottony armpits.

shadows have packed their bags and left.

villagersgather beneath tales of shade

as sun's jab daggers deep into their skins.

the drum explodes beneath the legs of memory,

with each yellowy nail burdened with the dirt of age.

a drunken stone catapulted through the brewery

staggers into the wrinkled behind of a century

where the drum is the ghost of the tree.

Places sadness shouldn't be

Grief

Soft-skinned senile sun

safely tucked in ash-grey clouds,

like I tucked you in that fateful night,

but unlike you,

Sun will rise again.

Death Next Door

Time drags the nightmare from under the bed.

Death's stride, absent rhythm,

strives to yank life from a brief, deep slumber:

that place all Nights hide in

when Sun for a wee bit reigns.

senescence sleeps for a while

in the abysm of our palms

and the breadth of our heavy arms

beneath the shadows that peddle the dark.

our foggy days drizzle in marshes

in which sun toils to wriggle her rays,

with her hands, strives to squeeze

drops of life from this our dry lemon.

yet, the wail floats in tiny ferryboats

to the coasts of our perpetual sunsets

and Death's visit next door

reminds us of when us Death did visit.

time drags the nightmare from under the bed

and our terror, renewed,

dares swallow dreams from our pillows –

a sister gone and a father buried.

The thing in funeral songs

The singing rolled out like a carpet

Grieving women had chewed the sad song,

and like the tears that died on their cheeks,

the song crawled down their faces:

Kudai magara pano, Razaro haaifa

The women's tears were not from

the hands that squeezed hearts like lemons,

nor in their voices,

unscathed by death's lashed claws,

but from the source of their song:

a woman here sang for a husband buried

in the depths of a crocodile's belly,

a mother there sang for a son

that went to buy tomatoes and never came back

Maria, usacheme Razaro achamuka

Death's silent stride

I squeezed ash out of moons.

I chewed light from Dawn's palms.

I sowed day in dewy mornings.

I laid father to rest in Dusk's teeth.

I milked air from withered leaves.

I lashed at Chance's skin with claws.

I burned Sun on my stove.

I watched through the window as sister died.

I shrunk time with bare hands.

I cut me a piece of night for supper.

I heard a faint knock on the door.

I did not see death come for me.

Fickle

came to me after the heat,

soft as a whisper imagined,

whistling past sun-scorched ears,

a gentle sigh leaving the mind to wonder:

Were you really here?

Muffled Voices

a wave of emotion rolled through her
like a surge of ungodly diseases.

the silence snapped like a stick,
and its two legs flew out of the room.

before dashing back through the window as one,
to kneel before the dry river below Mother's lip!

Valerie's Sonnets and other poems

The last person on earth

the day is a spent matchstick

her grey ashes, scattered across the blue

bestride our fallen shadows, and I, a cigarette long lit

seek her quavering lips beneath each rock

silent tree, to wise mountains

and old sea tides

and when we kiss the dark glitters

her laughter trapped in my mouth bounces

and melts into my smile –

for once we forget the silence

to focus on smoke marching above our cigarettes

which flares, burns swiftly and fades,

we watch water taste its own tastelessness

frown and laugh a little –

and you give out a laugh with sharp razor blades

sharpened into an everlasting face of the last rain.

Valerie's sonnet

When I drown my lungs in a pall of smoke
And breathing becomes a toil to my lungs,
When these lips loath vehemently idle talk
And silence ricochets like a bell loudly rung.

When lazy eyes catch a glimpse of my reflection
And see a rippling crowd of wrinkles on my skin
Quarrelling inaudibly about nature's decision,
To garb us with dust, and the people we've been.

Then I will know the time to leave is at hand
To a dwelling ruled by the repugnant night,
Neither sorrow nor terror should I befriend
For life and death have always been black and white.

Brave like the day I shall rise, ready to go
Happy that in Valerie my memories like kids will grow.

Young as the clock, old as time

When I recall the days of my youth
I perceive that I was not meant to grow old.
Hard as that tablet is to swallow, that pill is Truth,
For when these wrinkles came, the world grew cold.

In sorrow I lived when I was young
Knowing I'd never live to see my hair turn grey.
As food started to taste like rubber on my tongue,
To dross and dung turned all that was once gay.

While all around me turned to decay,
Valerie like a clock withstood the scourge of time;
Her body remained warm as summer's day,
And she as young as the clock and old as time:

In this war against Time, Time against me did cheat,
But my dear Valerie, like a clock suffered no defeat.

Mortal war

Even to the beauty of the red rose

Time doth lay siege, time and again.

The thought with strength in me arose:

That soon I'd leave, and Valerie would remain.

As if tears are sanitisers to the eyes,

When blurred I could finally clearly see

That time is constant, but it is I that flies,

And all that I am nowis all that I could ever be!

Yet thoughts of my death weigh not as heavy

As the thought of Valerie in another's arms.

Quickly forgotten, like I was but a scurvy,

And diseased were all my once sweet charms.

Yet, you are not, my love, the object of my rage,

But my mortal war with death I shall wage.

Dead but not gone

My father died in my brother's arms
With my mother weeping beside him.
Neither was night dim with death's charms
Nor did phlegmatic moon shed a tear for him.

Taverns drowned in drunken laughter
as drunkards kept at their usual games.
The whole world was still on the same chapter,
Even after my book had been set up in flames!

Valerie, let it not be so the day I am gone:
Summon them all whose hearts have loved,
And in memory of their loss, with you mourn
For me who only to you was truly beloved.

At last, in the dust I shall be alone,
dead, but not gone.

Sweet dreams

Jealous sleep has poisoned my eyes,
And with slumber I tumble to my bed,
But with the sun on the morrow I shall rise,
To see you as a rose beautiful and red.

What dreams may come when sight
Night has stolen could only be of you
Who rules my day and judges my night
Even after bidding each other adieu.

Then, day is like night and night like day
For when the senile sun goes down,
With its dying wish across the sky
You usurp its shimmering crown.

Therefore, when I close my eyes to sleep,
I know you'll be there, of my eternal sleep to weep.

Quest to quench love's thirst

My heart was a beggar's cup
Long used to receiving everyone's change.
Their pity and sympathy filled me up,
Until love seemed but an emotion so strange.

I was a fool to dream of it all the time,
Seeing it in the choral birds and naked skies
So much that it diseased even my rhyme,
And my poetry to my ears quickly became lies.

Long and deep I rummaged for a Muse,
Eager to make my verse once again true.
In such a search, all I had I would eventually lose
To become the greatest fool among all.

Yet, left with nothing to my name,
Your love came and covered my shame.

Seeds without number

You who has taught the flowers to bloom,

the bees to crop sweetness from their sweat,

the birds to sing songs scented as a perfumed room

and dawn with splendour from night to sprout,

You who sought to plant a Seed

in desert sands hellishly burning.

Of your efforts sand dunes made a ridicule,

and as madness your prayers were preyed upon.

Night time came dressed in polar temperatures,

And though your heart froze and ached for heat,

You were never heard to repine till Night's departure

With its tail tucked between its legs in defeat.

When the sun leapt from its slumber

Its one eye beheld the Seed become seeds without number.

Running the race

You in whom my life after life I have trusted

under a blind assumption that I will go first,

many a day and a night prayed I and fasted

that you be not served dust, before I dust had tasted.

yet haply God by my tears be moved not;

I'm persuaded to take matters into my own hands,

selfish as is love and wild as is this thought,

It is that which possesses me when I see the sands.

I rather you mourn me, than I weep over thee,

for whose tears are worthy to mourn a Muse?

Outlive me then and let me into eternal rest be,

for life was thrust upon me, but this ending I chose.

Therefore, my dear Valerie, to die I forbid you,

knowing my immortality depends on yours.

Scribbled words to immortality

Here, six feet in earth's heart, lies the writer,

his bones interred and memory forgotten.

Forgotten is how his fingers danced on a typewriter

on which his poesy lies serene and broken.

No echoes from the serried graves be heard,

just the silence the graveyard has married

to remind the gone that they're truly gone:

not that they need reminding – they're the buried!

Yet in that grave the writer twists and turns,

as his words scribbled in a bid for immortality

rot on brown pages in their thousands,

like dross and dung in an empty city.

For it is not the words that immortalise,

but Valerie who will read them, from dusk to sunrise.

The road to dust

tormented by forces I see not,
I see my fate wounded and dying.
like I was born without eyes, I cannot
see beyond the darkness surrounding.

some gods came to me in my sleep
and slipped in my mind terrors untold –
terrors that my mind intended not to keep –
that I was not meant to grow old.

my own shadow began to elude me
and my skin turned to a cloth of ash.
in that moment I finally knew me,
for all that was gold turned to trash.

but there's a darkness only the blind do see,
and in it I see Valerie rushing to save me.

Uncollected baggage

Between the mountain breasts

is a lonely river silently flowing

into the murky deep where water rests,

to flow free again only when dreaming.

Such a sorrowful scene seen briefly

by eyes blurred with misty thoughts

long cast to the solitude, carved neatly

from all humanity, to stand here distraught –

Here where nothing dares stand near me;

the earth is warm beneath my feet

while snow covers everything that be.

I carve me a chair from the wind to sit

yet time seems to circumvent me

as I close my eyes, hoping to never be.

buried whispers

beneath the midnight silence

is a song sung in a whisper

which I dare not ignore,

like a soft knock on my door.

I have been here before,

if not yesterday,

then a hundred years ago,

when the song bled out on the battlefield.

as the night turned to smoke and dust,

the song was shot in the gut

and its lyrics were its intestines.

silence, too terrified to stay, fled!

leaving bones of the whisper buried

where silence once lived.

a bed of thorns.

Valerie, among the untrodden ways

she dwelt among the untrodden ways:
betwixt a towering mountain's breasts,
like a tarn, silently chewing away her days,
a stranger to herself, and unknown to the rest.

Lost in my reveries, I climbed that mountain
where no feet had ever kissed,
to find between the rocks a warm fountain
in the perfect shape of Valerie's face.

Sun too tired, into slumber did fall,
and of my feet I made use,
hoping to return with Aurora's glow
to that place where my heart I'd left.

That mountain for years I did rummage
in search of a place I had been to,
and of this face I had seen,
to see only rocks and trees miles around.

of this Valerie, only memories remain,
a love known, never to be seen again.

(Her memories refuse to remain as such, softly crawling on my mind's walls, threatening
to catapult me back to the time Valerie and I were the horns of a bull: separated, yet ONE!)

My heart, scrubbing walls

(an apology)

On the footpath to tomorrow;
today has been lost,
among the grim grinder
green turned to grey.

the grim scent of yesterday's perfume
tumbles beneath today's clogged noses, roses
and day old daisies –
reek of soon to be lost days.
a morgue lashes loud old claws
smearing eternal silence with mortal wounds.

the thatched house of immoral excuses
catches fire on this execution
oh! death excuse me, I must blow my nose
for no one knows,
why the explanation gutted all good intentions!
This is not how it started,
her lips leapt into a violent kiss:
her breath was naked

her eyes were dressed and brazed in fire

and I was made of dry grass

her hips threw stones –

and I was made of glass.

precise strides,

time impales the pale thought.

my apology suffered impairment

so tomorrow is dead

and a stone was carved from its corpse,

today is forever long –

kidneys kidding skids urine back to the throat,

which throttles jolly juice in staffed joy tots,

spittle litters the tongue

in litres of liquefied words of regret

she wrung my tongue of its wet wrongs,

her hands were hammers

and I was a nail,

her voice was raging waters

and I was a snail,

her questions were hot knives,

and I was butter.

Bartered through

the veld fires blazed through the forest,

burned ash to life –

armpit hair fled to my mouth;

my words stank of a decade old sweat,

my reasons abysmal,

poisoned medicine whizzed from my tongue,

so I gave her my silence

and nailed my sorry eyes to the stained wall.

The Rest is Silence

An epoch of despair

It rained all week –
rolling billows of raging waters
swept Sun into rivers.

For forty nights
an army of droplets rattled roofs;

shattered windows screamed
and the waters mopped all sounds
with their freezing tongues.

New-borns cried silently,
their tongues drowned in the rain
that vowed to cut them from umbilical cords.

Fish and crabs crept into caves,
plants drowned,
and others grew old in obscure crevices.

Fishermen sew blankets from their nets,
made fire from their boats,
and bartered stories for dinner.

Harare Hospital (Ward four, four AM)

The guy on her left

Had tattoos on his chest.

When she woke up at four,

The guy had already left

Before they had given him his test results...

For those damn tests,

Four thousand dollars he paid,

And for four weeks on his bed he lay,

Waiting!

Waiting for a doctor to pronounce him dead!

Fight for life with a death that stutters

(after learning that she had tested positive for COVID-19)

ashes in my mouth!

what bitter taste ravages the senses

as a savage nausea churns my insides!

fear of being a statistic on tomorrow's news

pedals my clock anticlockwise

to an apocalyptic semi-real reality

where all lies beneath rubble

with blaring screams echoing.

another non-existing existence

where time circumvents me

until weary, it collapses on my knees:

to chime of my sister snapped

between death's carnivorous Jaws,

who with her last breath to me calls.

the smell of death

(Harare Hospital)

is antiseptics in the air at this hospital,

the stench of tarry faeces with blood,

Bled through the anus in a violent torrent

like the combustion of an old vehicle…

the scent of nurses bustling in the ward,

speaking in harsh hurried whispers,

as curtains are drawn when one is gone.

the odour of unwashed bodies,

and naked wounds with an army of pus,

slimy bastards sliding into the nose,

the perfume of new widows and orphans,

silently glaring at a future no longer there,

the smell of fervent prayers for healing,

whispered in the ears of the Forever Silent!

From behind the smoked glass

(after receiving the news that she could no longer speak)

Death's Jaws

soft as a whisper from a lover's treacherous lips,

gently strokes its prey with silent lullabies

sung from mists and gases

brought to the milky way from nebula,

a gothic prothalamion for an unholy marriage:

death and flesh helplessly tangled

 in an indissoluble embrace,

to give a turbid climax to a turgid megillah,

life's pendulum oscillating

from one form of death to another –

as the script is written,

the actress must ready to leave the stage…

Yet we would desire she tarries a little longer.

In the end, the end comes*

(when she spoke of her premonition)

...writes this from the
hospital.
wants it read when
she's gone.

knows this is the
end.
Her end.
didn't expect it to end
like this:

eyes sunken
lips shrunken
soul sulking
brains sullen

in her notebook
wrote,
"there I was,
here I am."

*For in the end, the end comes to put an end to us all, even though there seem
to be multiple endings to each story, there's only one end, the end that started
when we started on this stage. So, if life is indeed a stage, and dying an art, then
perhaps living is dying, and such is our performance before the curtain is drawn.

So this is dying? (Ndokufa kwacho nhai?)

(after learning that she had passed on)

echoes

bouncing on empty walls

back to their source,

before a misty silence

puts all to a double dead end.

Everything He gave

twice in value He has taken:

saka ndokufa kwacho nhai?

Insomnia

(The night after her death)

Sleep

      slips past my eyes

            as hope

                  hops into an inferno

                        with my bleeding heart

                          oh sweet sister

                              please

                                  come

                                      back!

A voice hung on spikes

(the same night)

When the noise fades
into a distant echo of what was,
terror crawls on my skin,
with a deathly life none has ever seen.

Your voice, though forever silent,
screams 'neath the weight of oblivion
burdened with words forever lost,
burned to ash, soon to be garbed in frost.

A maddening loneliness creeps
like snails sliding down slippery slopes.
When the screaming suddenly stops

it is then that I am made to know,
(what I have already known):
my dear sister is truly gone!

Seeing you again

(the day of her burial)

the tear drop in my eye

lingers to blur vision.

miles stretch upon miles,

a vast expanse expanding into

an infinite stretch of this moment.

the tear drop, last of its kind,

weeps with tears of its own,

for a brother who once had a sister

now shackled in this unpleasant present reality

where he stands alone.

within a few hours,

the tear drop falls sick and dies

leaving my eyes to see it all clearly:

there never was anything but this moment

I write about grief

(as her remains are laid to rest)

is a crown of thorns
laying siege to my heart,
making every breath
an act of simultaneously dying and living.

It is a hailstorm
of sharp nails shooting
at my eyeballs.

Grief is that witch,
casting deadly spells
to make this moment acid on my tongue,
taste like hairy armpits!

Grief is...
        Grief is that which is...
Grief is...

        ... "Killing me softly."

An infinite stretch

(the day after her burial)

Life

    is a wisp of steam

    dissipating

    from a boiling pot

    to memories of smoke,

    carving

    sense to create a void,

    toiling

    to become a black hole,

    howling

    to the other end

    of an endless stretch

    whose tether stretches,

    from life to death.

It was mine, it is not I

(A few days later)

williwaws from the mountain's face
surfing on her watery grave
made so by our mortal teary race

for her who's now eternally asleep,
the wailing twirls with whirling winds
and the haemorrhage runs deep

time demands her temple be decomposed
yet her bones, refusing to be interred,
command that this rhyme be composed.

its lyrics trapped in a lyre, stranger to glee,
turn to heaps of dust, piling to form memories
of a soul once trapped in flesh, now free –

for the body was indeed hers,
but that thing was never Her.

(title and the last couplet was inspired by Edwin Arnold, He Who Died at Azan, as reported in Hoyt's New Cyclopedia Of Practical Quotations, 1922)

What death is

dust gathers on the soles of her soul,

a brazen statue now poverty in virtue,

a gorgon caricature precisely captured

for the amusement of the ghostly circus

that paid a prostitute's fair market value

of thirty pieces of silver and Judas' kiss.

sullen eyes, sun's brilliance once beamed,

now the grim shadow of shattered mirrors,

comeliness absent, careless ugliness pregnant

in Sisyphean labours travailing pain to birth.

from between parted thighs chaos crawls,

as dust merges with the clothes she wears.

in futility the living ever so fertile,

only too glad of her to quickly forget!

(That's what death is, isn't it? Forgetting. Being forgotten. [Samwell Tarley, Game of Thrones, Season 8, Episode 2).

The rest is silence

serried graves carried hurried whispers,

sick words garbed in soiled diapers.

married folks in a bad joke

better than with a tombstone, idle talk?

anticlockwise wisely goes the clock,

wildly scuttling back to unknown o'clock

where the hour hand amputates time.

between *Then and now*

the fears take a humble bow;

the uptake of knowledge two breaths too late

but on the shoulders still heavy

as the thread sewn

to bind the *was never broken!*

coffee with the venerated Pope,

among death wishes squats at the top.

cobwebs in the mouth,

the tongue a decaying rope,

words in a cat's straggle

struggle to parade to form meaningful sentences:

you were wrong, oh clergy,

silence is another form of noise!

flesh dashed and cashed in both our time,

in search of noise, riotously spent what's mine.

so here I lie, still as the cerulean sky,

as the pottery that turned to poetry.

God's wounds drip pus of gold

on dusty bones like a dinner served cold.

time is a dislocated joint.

nine months shut in the womb

devoid of intelligible speech just like in the tomb,

yet on arrival the wise child speaks wisdom,

in deafening screams, grasped not by the audience:

the rest is silence.

The missing bard

time, as if wounded, crawls beneath the door,

coughs three decades, and coughs no more.

The terror of the Bard's death

I hated to live.

my grief

burned my veins into ash.

eyes bruised,

and vision blurred,

screamed the terror into life in my head.

I murdered the tick of the clock,

with bare hands strangled rivers.

I rattled the moon,

stabbed dank clouds that wept dust.

night fled and hid behind the sun.

I poked sun's one eye

and oceans churned into empty space,

land trembled beneath my feet

and air tumbled to its knees:

all this did I in my head

for the Ancient Bard was dead

Acknowledgements

Samantha Vazhure and the Carnelian Heart Publishing company took a great risk in publishing my work. A risk not many would take given the nature of the market for poetry books right now. But they did it anyway, and for that I am grateful. Under the same bracket I would like to thank Marie Christie for beta reading my work, Memory Chirere for editing this collection, Tanaka Chidora for the foreword, and Obey Chiyangwa for telling me that I could write!

My desire to write poetry would have been nothing without the ability to do so. How long I tittered in the shadows, afraid to take up a pen and speak! As a young lad in high school, I wrote a few hundred works of poetry that had neither the words nor the meaning to make them worthy pieces. But they helped me shape myself into a stone. The poems were free, happy and could transform in ways I could never do now! My gratitude goes to my best friend Matthew Chikono, who not having the modicum of knowledge of what poetry ought to be, read each of those pieces like they were the words of Wordsworth himself!

My poetry would take a significant turn when I met Tanaka Chidora in 2018. By that time I had enrolled at the University of Zimbabwe majoring in Accounting. I was beginning to make use of the university's special collections section. My poetry could not remain immune to the works I was reading; it got better in delivery but terrible in identity. Each poem was an awkward mixture of influences from Dambudzo Marechera to Sylvia Path.

Meeting Dr Chidora altered my path. He brought to me the confidence necessary to write in my own voice and skin. He brought freedom and identity to my work. He remained instrumental in the publication of this book, in ways I cannot explain and for that Tanaka; I am truly grateful

I would like to also thank Letricia Matanda for her contribution to the "Kathy poems" in this book. While Kathy's identity will remain a mystery to both of us, I know in many ways, you and I gave birth to the idea of what Kathy has become, and for that thank you, 7!

Thank you to Onai Mushava for giving me the chance to call myself a writer by publishing my first poetry collection, Andrew Kahari for the input that made this collection and many others whose names may not have been mentioned but whose contribution is a great part of this collection.

About the author

Tafadzwa Chiwanza is a writer and an auditor with Deloitte. His work has been published in This Is Africa, The Herald, NewsDay, The Standard, NewsHawks and other newspapers. He is also the author of *No Bird is Singing Now?* (2020).

9 781914 287794